Informing the legislative debate since 1914

Medal of Honor: History and Issues

David F. Burrelli
Specialist in Military Manpower Policy

Barbara Salazar Torreon
Information Research Specialist

September 5, 2014

Congressional Research Service

7-5700

www.crs.gov

95-519

Summary

The Medal of Honor is the nation's highest military award for bravery. It is awarded by the President in the name of Congress. For this reason, it is often referred to as the Congressional Medal of Honor. Since it was first presented in 1863, the medal has been awarded 3,507 times to 3,488 recipients. Nineteen individuals have been double recipients of the award.

Recipients of the Medal of Honor are afforded a number of benefits as a result of this award.

Since the award's inception, the laws and regulations that apply to it have changed. In certain cases, the award has been rescinded. Six rescinded awards have been reinstated.

On a number of occasions, legislation has been offered to waive certain restrictions and to encourage the President to award the Medal of Honor to particular individuals. Generally speaking, this type of legislation is rarely enacted. In a very limited number of cases, the medal has been awarded outside the legal restrictions concerning time limits. These cases are often based on technical errors, lost documents or eyewitness accounts, or other factors that justify reconsideration. These cases, however, represent the exception and not the rule.

For information on recent recipients, see CRS Report RL30011, *Medal of Honor Recipients: 1979-2013*, by Anne Leland.

Contents

Tables

Appendixes

Contacts

Members and staff of Congress often ask the Congressional Research Service to provide information concerning the awarding of the Medal of Honor (MoH). This report briefly describes the history of the MoH and the criteria and rules used in awarding the medal. The benefits that are made available to Medal of Honor recipients are listed. This report also describes the process involved in reconsidering an individual for receipt of the medal (including what assistance a Member may provide in this process). The applicable statutes concerning those improperly holding, trading, or selling the award as well as those who wrongly claim to be medal recipients are summarized. Some citations of those who have been awarded the MoH are provided as examples including the most recent recipient, Army Sergeant Ryan M. Pitts, on July 21, 2014, along with certain statistics describing the recipients. For more information on recent recipients, see CRS Report RL30011, *Medal of Honor Recipients: 1979-2013*, by Anne Leland.

Background

According to a U.S. Senate Committee Print on the Medal of Honor:

> The Medal of Honor is the highest award for bravery[1] that can be given to any individual in the United States of America. Conceived in the early 1860's and first presented in 1863, the medal has a colorful and inspiring history which has culminated in the standards applied today for awarding this respected honor.
>
> In their provisions for judging whether a man is entitled to the Medal of Honor, each of the armed services has set up regulations which permit no margin of doubt or error. The deed of the person must be proved by incontestable evidence of at least two eyewitnesses; it must be so outstanding that it clearly distinguishes his gallantry beyond the call of duty from lesser forms of bravery; it must involve the risk of his life; and it must be of the type of deed which, if he had not done it, would not subject him to any justified criticism.
>
> A recommendation for the Army or Air Force Medal must be made within 2 years from the date of the deed upon which it depends. Award of the medal must be made within 3 years after the date of the deed. The recommendation for a Navy Medal of Honor must be made within 3 years and awarded within 5 years.
>
> Apart from the great honor which it conveys, there are certain small privileges which accompany the Medal of Honor....
>
> The Medal of Honor is presented to its recipients by a high official "in the name of the Congress of the United States." For this reason it is sometimes called the Congressional Medal of Honor.
>
> As a general rule, the Medal of Honor can be earned—by a deed of personal bravery or self-sacrifice above and beyond the call of duty—only while a person is a member of the American Armed Forces in actual combat with an enemy of the Nation. This was the case,

---

[1] Acts of bravery and courage are not unusual among those in uniform. The fact that many members of the U.S. Armed Forces have engaged in direct battle with an enemy or carried out their duties under enemy attack is taken as a sign of this bravery and courage. However, the level of heroism usually cited among those who receive the Medal of Honor is uncommonly high and of a qualitatively different magnitude. The distinction of this type of valor, heroism, courage, and bravery, in an environment where bravery and courage are the norm—and must be the norm in order to carry out effective military operations—may prove difficult to recognize by the outsider.

for example, during World Wars I and II and the Korean conflict. However, the Navy Medal of Honor could be and has been on several occasions, awarded to noncombatants.

On a few, rare occasions, the Congress of the United States has awarded special Medals of Honor for individual exploits taking place in peacetime. Such a Medal of Honor was awarded Capt. Charles A. Lindbergh for his "heroic courage and skill as a navigator, at the risk of his life, for his nonstop flight in his airplane from New York to Paris, France, 20-21 May 1927." In peace or war, this medal is the highest decoration which can be given in any of the Armed Forces—Army, Navy, Marine Corps, Air Force, or Coast Guard.[2]

Since its beginning, the awarding of the Medal of Honor has been subjected to numerous changes. Although not the first award,[3] the medal became very popular. Cases of abuse, wherein soldiers obtained the award surreptitiously and used it to solicit charity, have been cited.

As of this printing, 3,507 Medals of Honor have been awarded to 3,488 recipients. There have been 19 double recipients (14 for separate actions and five cases in which the Army and Navy Medals of Honor were awarded for the same action). Since World War I, there has been an implied reluctance to award the medal more than once to the same person.

During the Civil War, President Lincoln, in need of troops, awarded the medal to the members of a single regiment (the 27th Maine Volunteer Infantry), as an inducement to keep them on active duty. Due to a clerical error, the entire unit (864 men) received the medal, despite the fact that only 309 men actually volunteered for extended duty (the rest went home). Others were awarded the medal under questionable circumstances. William F. (Buffalo Bill) Cody and others were awarded the medal although they were civilians serving with the military. Mary Edwards Walker, a contract surgeon (civilian) and the only woman to receive the medal, was allegedly awarded it during the Civil War to placate her after the termination of her contract with the Army.[4] Questions of her medical skills and loyalties to the Union have been raised over the years (see p. 8).

In 1916, a board was created to determine eligibility for the award and to review the cases of those who had already received the award:

> And in any case ... in which said board shall find and report that said medal was issued for any cause other than that hereinbefore specified the name of the recipient of the medal so issued shall be stricken permanently from the official Medal of Honor list. It shall be a misdemeanor for him to wear or publicly display such medal, and, if he shall be in the Army, he shall be required to return said medal to the War Department for cancellation.[5]

All of the 2,625 medals awarded up to that time were considered by the board, and nearly one-third (911) were canceled. Most of these canceled awards constituted those issued to the 27th Maine Volunteer Infantry. William Cody's and Mary Edwards Walker's awards were canceled.

---

[2] U.S. Congress, Senate Committee on Labor and Public Welfare, Subcommittee on Veterans' Affairs, *Medal of Honor 1863-1968*, 90th Cong., 2d sess. (Washington: GPO, 1968), p. 1. For a list of recent recipients and their citations, see CRS Report RL30011, *Medal of Honor Recipients: 1979-2013*, by Anne Leland.

[3] George Washington created the Purple Heart in 1782. Three men received the award in 1783. The Purple Heart was not awarded again until World War I or later, and has been based on different criteria.

[4] Rudi Williams, "Only Woman Medal of Honor Holder Ahead of Her Time," American Forces Press Service, April 30, 1999, at http://www.defense.gov/News/NewsArticle.aspx?ID=42772

[5] *Medal of Honor*, Committee Print, 1968, p. 9.

In 1918, during U.S. participation in World War I, Congress decided to clear away any inconsistencies of the legislation which had grown around the Army medal and make a set of perfectly clear rules for its award....

> [T]he provisions of existing law relating to the award of the Medals of Honor ... are amended so that the President is authorized to present, in the name of Congress, a Medal of Honor only to each person who, while an officer or enlisted man of the Army, shall hereafter, in action involving actual conflict with an enemy, distinguish himself conspicuously by gallantry and intrepidity at risk of his life above and beyond the call of duty.[6]

Policies, regulations and guidance were provided to commanders throughout the following years concerning the medal for the Army as well as the other services. In many ways, these later awards were better documented. Such documentation served as a standard for the consideration of other deeds in awarding the Medal of Honor or other appropriate awards (i.e., the Silver Star, Bronze Star, etc.). Examples of citations of Medal of Honor awards from various periods are included in the appendix and in CRS Report RL30011, *Medal of Honor Recipients: 1979-2013*, by Anne Leland.

Under current law:

> The President may award, and present in the name of Congress, a medal of honor of appropriate design, with ribbons and appurtenances, to a person who while a member of the Army [Naval Service—i.e., Navy, Marine Corps and Coast Guard, or Air Force], distinguishes himself conspicuously by gallantry and intrepidity at the risk of his life above and beyond the call of duty—
>
> (1) while engaged in military operations against an enemy of the United States;
>
> (2) while engaged in military operations involving conflict with an opposing foreign force; or,
>
> (3) while serving with friendly foreign forces engaged in an armed conflict against an opposing armed force in which the United States is not a belligerent party.[7]

Current Policy and Benefits

The following information is from the Department of Defense (DOD) *Manual of Military Decorations & Awards*.[8]

---

[6] *Medal of Honor*, Committee Print, 1968, p. 11.

[7] Title 10, *U.S. Code*, Sec. 3741, Aug. 10, 1956, ch. 1041, 70A Stat. 215; July 25, 1963, P.L. 88-77, Sec. 1(1), 77 Stat. 93; Sec. 6241, Aug. 10, 1956, ch. 1041, 70A Stat. 389; July 25, 1963, P.L. 88-77, Sec. 2(1), 77 Stat. 93; and, Sec. 8741, Aug. 10, 1956, ch. 1041, 70A Stat. 540; July 25, 1963, P.L. 88-77, Sec. 3(1), 77 Stat. 93. Title 10 also allows the President to delegate his authority to award the Medal of Honor. Thus, the authority to award the Medal lies with the President alone unless he so delegates others to do so in his place.

[8] U.S. Department of Defense, *Manual of Military Decorations & Awards*, DoD 1348.33-M, November 23, 2010, Incorporating Change 3, July 10, 2014, at http://www.dtic.mil/whs/directives/corres/pdf/134833vol1.pdf

Procedures Involving Recommendations for the MoH

[1.] The Secretary concerned shall establish procedures for processing recommendations for the award of the MoH in his or her Military Department. Minimally, those recommendations shall contain the endorsement of the subordinate Unified Combatant Commander or the JTF Commander, if involved; the Unified Combatant Commander concerned; and the Chairman of the Joint Chiefs of Staff. After endorsement by the Chairman of the Joint Chiefs of Staff, the recommendation shall be referred to the Secretary concerned for appropriate action.

[2.] The Army and Air Force MoH recommendations must be entered formally into official channels in two years of the act warranting the recommendation, and awarded in three years (except as provided in title 10 U.S.C. 3744 or 8744 ... and Section 1130 of title 10, U.S.C.... The Navy-Marine Corps MoH recommendations must be formally entered into official channels in three years of the act warranting the recommendation, and awarded in five years.... However, a Member of Congress can request consideration of a proposal for the award or presentation of a decoration not previously submitted in a timely fashion....

[3.] Recommendations for award of the MoH disapproved by a Secretary of a Military Department, or Secretary of Defense, may only be resubmitted if new, substantive and material information is provided in the time limits.... The information forming the basis must have been previously unknown and not considered by the recommending and disapproving officials. The determination of the existence of the new material and substantive information being a basis for reconsideration may not be delegated below the Service Secretary.

[a.] The remaining bases for reconsideration are instances in which a Secretary of a Military Department or the Secretary of Defense determines there is evidence of material error or impropriety in the original processing of or decision on a recommendation for award of the MoH. Examples of such instances might be loss of accompanying and/or substantiating documents to the recommendation or proven gender or racial discrimination. Determination of the existence of material error or impropriety in the original processing and decision shall not be delegated below the Secretary of a Military Department. In such cases, the Secretary of Defense shall determine the need for legislation.

[b.] All other instances of reconsideration shall be limited to those in which the formal recommendation was submitted in statutory time limits, the recommendation was lost or inadvertently not acted upon, and when these facts are conclusively established by the respective Secretary of a Military Service or other official delegated appropriate authority. Those provisions are to protect the integrity and purity of purpose of the MoH by ensuring that all relevant information is submitted and considered while the actions are fresh in the minds of the witnesses.

The process for restoration of a rescinded Medal of Honor is different. Since the rescissions during World War I, no other MoH awards have been rescinded. However, if a request for a restoration of a MoH were made, the process would be different than the procedures noted above. For those seeking restoration of the Medal of Honor, an appeal must be considered by the appropriate Board for Correction of Military Records.[9] This appeal is requested via the President,

---

[9] DoD Knowledge Base, Contact information for the Boards for Correction of Military Records for each of the services at https://kb.defense.gov/app/answers/detail/a_id/386/~/boards-for-correction-of-military-records. A link to DD Form 149, Application for Correction of Military Records under the Provisions of Title 10, U.S. Code, Section 1552, is provided.

a Member of Congress, or the Secretary of Defense. If the board recommends reinstatement, the decision is passed to the service Secretary and then, ultimately, to the President.

Presentation of the MoH

When practical, presentation of the MoH shall be made by the President of the United States, as CINC [Commander-in-Chief], in a formal ceremony in Washington, D.C. As such, premature public disclosure of information concerning recommendations, processing and approval or disapproval actions is a potential source of embarrassment to those recommended and the Government. Additionally, in the case of approved recommendations, it could diminish the impact of ceremonies at which the presentation is made. Therefore, to prevent premature disclosure, the policy of the Department is not to comment on any MoH case under consideration. Accordingly, the processing of MoH recommendations shall be handled on a "FOR OFFICIAL USE ONLY" basis until the awards are announced officially or are presented.

Courtesies and Privileges Afforded MoH Recipients

[1.] Each recipient receives a monthly [1,277.89] dollar pension from the Department of Veterans Affairs (VA).[10]

[2.] Enlisted recipients who retire with 20 or more years of Military Service receive a 10-percent increase in retired pay, not to exceed the 75 percent maximum.

[3.] Recipients are issued a special MoH Travel and Identification Card signed by the Secretary of the Military Department. That entitles recipients who are not on active duty and not military retirees to use space available military air transportation.

[4.] Unlike [active duty and reserve] military personnel and retirees, MoH recipients may wear their uniforms at any time or place they choose.

[5.] Recipients who are not on active duty and not military retirees are issued a DoD Identification Card, as are their family members. It authorizes them military commissary, post exchange, and theater privileges. All of the Services, consistent with DoD policy, authorize use of morale, welfare and recreation activities, including honorary club membership without dues.

[6.] Children of MoH recipients are not subject to quotas if they are qualified and desire to attend one of the U.S. military academies.

[7.] MoH recipients receive invitations to attend Presidential inaugurations and accompanying festivities. Military recipients and those who are civil servants have traditionally been authorized administrative absence in lieu of chargeable leave to attend.

---

[10] The Veterans Benefits Act of 2002 (P.L. 107-330) created a formula for future increases in the Medal of Honor pension tied to the annual rate of inflation. Previously, each increase in the Medal of Honor pension occurred as a result of an act of Congress. See CRS Report RS22804, *Veterans' Benefits: Pension Benefit Programs*, by Umar Moulta-Ali and Carol D. Davis, "Medal of Honor Pension" on p.7; and the Department of Veterans Affairs, Special Benefit Allowances Rates: Current as of December 1, 2013, at http://www.benefits.va.gov/compensation/special_Benefit_Allowances_2013.asp

[8.] The VA provides a special engraved headstone for deceased recipients of the MoH.

[9.] MoH recipients should be accorded on-base billeting commensurate with the prestige associated with the MoH.

In 2000, Congress extended permissive health care benefits to Medal of Honor recipients and their dependents in the same manner as is currently available to military retirees and their dependents.[11]

In addition, they receive a 10% increase in retired pay up to 75% of active duty pay (10 U.S.C. §3991, See sub (a) (2)):

> (2) ADDITIONAL 10 PERCENT FOR CERTAIN ENLISTED MEMBERS CREDITED WITH EXTRAORDINARY HEROISM.—If a member who is retired under section 3914 of this title has been credited by the Secretary of the Army with extraordinary heroism in the line of duty, the member's retired pay shall be increased by 10 percent of the amount determined under paragraph (1) (but not more than 75 percent of the retired pay base upon which the computation of such retired pay is based). The Secretary's determination as to extraordinary heroism is conclusive for all purposes.

Congressional and Other Efforts to Award the Medal of Honor

Generally speaking, the originating request for military awards, including the MoH, is made by the military commander or other appropriate uniformed personnel. Those on the scene and/or those familiar with military operations are often considered to be in the best position to observe the individual actions and make the recommendation for award. It is considered appropriate, therefore, that military personnel—that is, those familiar with human behavior under the stress of combat situations—make the originating recommendations regarding this or other awards.

In a number of instances, Members of Congress or others have urged the President to consider or reconsider an individual for the MoH. Over the years, Members of Congress have offered numerous bills for this purpose. Much of this legislation takes the form of extensive findings detailing the background, situation, and exploits concerned. Where important, special mention may be made of the reason(s) the MoH was not originally awarded (e.g., a presumption of racism, lost documents recently uncovered, etc.). The legislation then resolves that notwithstanding restrictions contained in Title 10 U.S.C. (i.e., restrictions pertaining to time limits), the President is "requested" to award the MoH.[12] In certain cases, Congress has held hearings concerning the award.[13] See **Table 1** for a list of MoH bills introduced during the 113th Congress.

---

[11] P.L. 106-398; 114 Stat. 1654, 1654A-175; October 30, 2000.

[12] For examples of legislation offered in the 113th Congress, see H.R. 658, H.R. 1237, H.R. 2082, H.R. 2106, H.R. 3304, H.R. 3364, H.Con.Res. 26, S. 993, S. 1258, and S.Con.Res. 9

[13] See U.S. Congress, House Armed Services Committee, Subcommittee on Personnel and Compensation, *H.J.Res. 279, H.R. 1730, and H.R. 3401 (Vraciu Congressional Medal of Honor and MIAs/KIAs)*, HASC No. 101-77, 101st Cong., 2d Sess., January 30, 1990; cited from opening statement provided at the hearing.

Table 1. Medal of Honor Bills in the 113th Congress (2013-2014)

Bill Number and Date Introduced	Title	Latest Action
H.R. 658 on 2/13/2013	To authorize and request the President to award the congressional Medal of Honor to Arthur Jibilian for actions behind enemy lines during World War II while a member of the United States Navy and the Office of Strategic Services.	2/28/2013 - Referred to the House Subcommittee on Military Personnel.
H.R. 1237 on 3/18/2013	To authorize and request the President to award the Medal of Honor posthumously to Major Dominic S. Gentile of the United States Army Air Forces for acts of valor during World War II.	4/8/2013 - Referred to the House Subcommittee on Military Personnel.
H.R. 2082 on 5/21/2013	Private Bill; To authorize and request the President to award the Medal of Honor to James Megellas, formerly of Fond du Lac, Wisconsin, and currently of Colleyville, Texas, for acts of valor on January 28, 1945, during the Battle of the Bulge in World War II.	6/20/2013 – Referred to the House Subcommittee on Military Personnel.
H.R. 2106 on 5/22/2013	To authorize and request the President to award the Medal of Honor posthumously to First Lieutenant Alonzo H. Cushing for acts of valor during the Civil War.	6/20/2013 - Referred to the House Subcommittee on Military Personnel.
H.R. 3304 on 10/22/2013	National Defense Authorization Act (NDAA) for Fiscal Year 2014 Subtitle H, Section 583 – regarding standardization to time limits for Recommending and Awarding MOH, DSC, NC, AFC, DSM; Section 584 – recodification and revision of MOH requirements; Section 587 – MOH consideration for Sgt. Rafael Peralta; Section 588 – DSC for Sgt Robert F. Kreiser, Korean War.	12/26/2013 – Became Public Law No: 113-66. See the following: Sec. 561. Repeal of limitation on number of medals; Sec. 562. Standardization of time-limits for recommending and awarding Medal of Honor and other medals; Sec. 563. Recodification and revision of Medal of Honor Roll requirements. Sec. 566. Authorization for award of the Medal of Honor to former members of the Armed Forces previously recommended for award of the Medal of Honor. Sec. 567. Authorization for award of the Medal of Honor for acts of valor during the Vietnam War. Sec. 569. Authorization for award of the Medal of Honor to First Lieutenant Alonzo H. Cushing for acts of valor during the Civil War.

Bill Number and Date Introduced	Title	Latest Action
H.R. 3364 on 10/29/2013	To authorize and request the President to issue a posthumous commission in the regular Army to Milton Holland, who, while sergeant major of the 5th Regiment, United States Colored Infantry, was awarded the Medal of Honor for gallantry during the Civil War.	1/24/2014 Referred to the House Subcommittee on Military Personnel.
H.R. 4233 on 3/13/2014	To authorize the President to award the Medal of Honor posthumously to Lance Corporal Jordan C. Haerter and Corporal Jonathan Yale of the Marine Corps for acts of valor during Operation Iraqi Freedom in April 2008.	3/13/2014 - Referred to the House Committee on Armed Services.
H.R. 5302 on 7/30/2014	Private Bill; To authorize the President to award the Medal of Honor to Special Forces Command Sergeant Major Ramon Rodriguez of the United States Army for acts of valor during the Vietnam War.	7/30/2014- Referred to the House Committee on Armed Services.
H.Con.Res. 26 on 3/19/2013	Recommending the posthumous award of the Medal of Honor to Sergeant Rafael Peralta.	4/5/2013 Referred to the House Subcommittee on Military Personnel.
S. 993 on 5/21/2013	A bill to authorize and request the President to award the Medal of Honor to James Megellas, formerly of Fond du Lac, Wisconsin, and currently of Colleyville, Texas, for acts of valor on January 28, 1945, during the Battle of the Bulge in World War II.	6/4/2013 Referred to the Senate Committee on Armed Services by unanimous consent.
S. 1258 on 6/27/2013	A bill to authorize and request the President to award the Medal of Honor posthumously to First Lieutenant Alonzo H. Cushing for acts of valor during the Civil War.	6/27/2013 Referred to the House Subcommittee on Military Personnel.
S.Con.Res. 9 on 3/19/2013	A concurrent resolution recommending the posthumous award of the Medal of Honor to Sergeant Rafael Peralta.	3/19/2013 Referred to Senate Committee. Status: Referred to the Committee on Armed Services.

Source: Legislative Information System (LIS) at http://www.congress.gov.

The handling of these requests, if and when forwarded to the services, varies depending on whether the individual was originally recommended for the Medal of Honor (or in certain cases, had already received the medal), versus those instances in which no original recommendation was made.

Generally speaking, the services will not favorably consider awarding the MoH unless the individual was originally recommended but did not receive the award because of extenuating circumstances (e.g., the paperwork was lost and only rediscovered, allegations exist that the individual's award was downgraded for reasons of racism, etc.). In nearly every case, specific findings of fact are required that the individual was originally recommended or that the downgrade occurred under questionable, but verifiable, circumstances. In these cases, a review may be undertaken by the Board of Correction for Military Records (BCMR) of the appropriate military department.[14] Following the findings of the BCMR, the decision is then passed to appropriate authorities for further and/or final consideration. This approach has not usually been successful.

In cases where no original recommendation has been made, extensive and reliable findings of valid facts must be presented. In these instances, since there is no original record to "correct," the BCMR is not necessarily involved in the consideration process. Without an original recommendation, factual data supporting the award, and compelling reasons for it to be awarded at a later date, it is very unlikely that the MoH will be awarded. This is particularly so, given that a great deal of time has often passed and eyewitnesses cannot be found, or do not clearly remember the events in question.

Nevertheless, on numerous occasions, legislation has been introduced seeking to have the MoH awarded. The legislation is assigned to the appropriate committee/subcommittee. An executive comment is usually requested by the committee. In most cases, the executive comment proves unfavorable and the legislation is not reported out of committee.

In recent times, there have been a number of specific instances in which the MoH was awarded or reinstated outside of the statutory time limits. In one case, the award was renounced. The following are examples of these instances.

For his actions in Vietnam on May 2, 1968, MSgt. Roy Benavidez, U.S. Army, was awarded the Distinguished Service Cross (the second-highest Army award for heroism below the MoH). His commander later recommended that the award be upgraded to the Medal of Honor. The upgrade was denied until a missing eyewitness was located in 1980. President Carter approved the upgrade on December 31, 1980. On February 24, 1981, President Reagan awarded MSgt. Benavidez the MoH.[15]

The family of Marine Col. Donald G. Cook (deceased) received his MoH award on May 16, 1980, for his services during captivity as a POW in North Vietnam from December 31, 1964 through his death in captivity on December 8, 1967. Information of his heroics was only obtained after the repatriation of other POWs. Col. Cook's award was delayed in part because he had not been officially declared dead.[16]

President Carter awarded the medal to former Army Lt. Col. Matt Urban for his services during World War II. Urban's battalion commander promised to nominate him for the award but was killed in action. A review of Urban's records in 1978 revealed a copy of the proposed letter. There is no evidence, however, that the letter was received by the headquarters of the 9th Infantry

---

[14] DOD Knowledge Base, Boards for Correction of Military Records at https://kb.defense.gov/app/answers/detail/a_id/386/~/boards-for-correction-of-military-records.

[15] Don Hirst, "Benavidez Receives Medal of Honor," *Army Times*, March 9, 1981, p. 34. Congress enacted P.L. 96-81 on December 18, 1980, removing the statutory time limit on the award, thereby clearing the way for MSgt. Benavidez to receive the medal.

[16] "Colonel Awarded Medal of Honor Posthumously," *Navy Times*, May 26, 1980, p. 2.

Division in Europe. Under the provisions of the law, a President can make the final decision of awarding the medal "at any later time in cases of administrative error."[17]

On July 29, 1986, Charles Liteky, a former Army chaplain in Vietnam, renounced his Medal of Honor in protest over U.S. policies in Central America. Liteky's is the only known case in which a Medal of Honor has been renounced.[18]

On April 24, 1991, President George H.W. Bush awarded the MoH (posthumously) to Cpl. Freddie Stowers, U.S. Army, for his services in World War I. Although blacks had received the award for other conflicts before and since, Stowers was, at the time, the only black to be awarded the MoH for either World War. This presentation followed a review of the award by the Army into citation records to determine whether or not blacks were treated fairly.[19]

Perhaps one of the more contentious awarding of the Medal of Honor involved the case of the Civil War civilian contract surgeon Mary Edwards Walker. She was awarded the Medal of Honor by President Andrew Johnson on November 11, 1865, for "services rendered during the war." She was a flamboyant and controversial character, and it has been argued that the award was made to placate her for being terminated by the Army. As with certain other medal recipients of her day, no specific act of heroism was cited for receiving it.[20] Under the review panel's considerations, Dr. Walker's award was stricken because she was not a member of the Armed Forces and because her services did not involve "actual conflict with an enemy, by gallantry or intrepidity, at the risk of life, above and beyond the call of duty."

At the behest of distant relatives, some Members of Congress and President Carter contacted the Department of Defense on the matter. The Army Board for Corrections of Military Records ruled (with one dissent) that the decision to rescind the award was "unjust." Although the board noted that if it had not been for her sex, she would have been given a commission and her actions would have been those of a soldier, no specific act of gallantry or heroism was noted. In 1977, her medal was restored. The restoration of the medal remains highly contentious among both proponents and opponents of this action.[21]

On September 12, 1980, President Carter awarded Anthony Casamento, a Marine Corps veteran of combat against the Japanese on Guadalcanal during World War II, the Medal of Honor. Lacking sufficient witnesses to attest to certain deeds, military officials argued that Casamento should be awarded only the Navy Cross. The President overruled the Pentagon (including the Secretary of Defense) and awarded the MoH. Critics contend that President Carter's action was timed for political effect, as the President awarded the medal just prior to an election-year appearance before the National Italian-American Foundation.[22]

---

[17] Chip Brown, "Medal of Honor Winners: 203 Certified Heroes Here: A Pantheon of Certified Heroes Gather," *Washington Post*, January 19, 1981, p. C3.

[18] "Veteran Returns Medal to Protest U.S. Policy," *Washington Post*, July 30, 1986, p. B3.

[19] "Medal of Honor for Black G.I.," *New York Times*, April 6, 1991: 6.

[20] In fact, numerous interpretations of her service record raise questions regarding her skills and loyalty. Others have charged that these claims were the result of rampant sexism. Allen D. Spiegel and Andrea M. Spiegel, "Civil War Doctoress Mary: Only Woman to Win Congressional Medal of Honor," *Minerva: Quarterly Report on Women and the Military*, vol. XIII, no. 3, Fall 1994, p. 25.

[21] See Gene Famiglietti, "MH Award to Dr. Walker Is Hit," *Army Times*, June 1977, p. 4; and Nick Adde, "Real American Heroes," *Army Times*, April 11, 1988, p. 57.

[22] Rowland Evans and Robert Novak, "Playing Politics with the Pentagon," *Washington Post*, September 12, 1980, p. (continued...)

Following the example of the reinstatement of the award to Dr. Walker, relatives of William F. "Buffalo Bill" Cody sought reinstatement of his medal, in part on the grounds that since Dr. Walker's was reinstated, there existed a precedent for awarding the medal to civilians who served with the military. Cody was originally awarded the Medal of Honor on May 22, 1872, for his gallantry while serving as an Army Scout on April 26, 1872, at the Platte River, Nebraska. At the request of a U.S. Senator serving as the counsel for a relative, the Board for Correction of Military Records recommended reinstatement of "Buffalo Bill" Cody's medal, citing in part the award of Dr. Walker.[23] In June 1989, the U.S. Army Board of Correction of Military Records restored the award, and on July 8, 1989, two Senators announced the restoration of Cody's medal.[24] (Four others also had their medals reinstated by the board in June 1989: Amos Chapman [Scout], William Dixon [Scout], James B. Doshier [Post Guide], and William H. Woodall [Scout].)[25]

Throughout the years, many efforts to award or reinstate the Medal of Honor have proven time-consuming and difficult. For example, advocates for Seaman Doris (a.k.a. Dorie or Dorrie) Miller have sought for years to have his award upgraded to the Medal of Honor. During the Japanese attack on Pearl Harbor on December 7, 1941, while serving aboard the *USS West Virginia* as a mess attendant (one of the only jobs available to blacks in the Navy at the beginning of World War II), Seaman Miller moved his mortally wounded captain to safety. He then proceeded to man a machine gun, successfully returning fire on the attacking Japanese. His heroics were initially ignored. After strong civil rights protests, he was given a letter of commendation. The letter of commendation was upgraded to the Navy Cross. A destroyer escort was later named in his honor. Legislative and other efforts to upgrade the Navy Cross to the Medal of Honor have proven unsuccessful. Noting that, at the time, no blacks received the Medal of Honor during WWII; critics cite racism as a main reason for refusing Seaman Miller this honor.

The reluctance to upgrade awards to the Medal of Honor or to award it outright is generally based on efforts to award the medal to those truly deserving, to maintain the integrity of the award itself and the awards process in general, and to avoid "opening the floodgates" to retroactive requests for this and other awards and decorations. This reluctance has led many to feel that the system of awarding medals is overly restrictive and that certain individuals are denied earned medals.

It is noteworthy that two MoH awards have gone "unclaimed."[26] A posthumous medal awarded to Navy Chief Peter Tomich in 1942 for heroism at Pearl Harbor was never claimed since there were no known relatives, and according to the Navy Museum curator, Edward M. Furgol, the 20th century produced at least one other unclaimed MoH from 1904.[27]

(...continued)

A19.

[23] U.S. Department of the Army, Board for the Correction of Military Records, Washington, D.C., In the Case of: Cody, William F., AC88-10374, January 12, 1989.

[24] "'Buffalo Bill' Regains Medal of Honor," *Washington Post*, July 9, 1989, p. A5.

[25] *United States of America's Congressional Medal of Honor Recipients and Their Official Citations*. Minnesota: Highland House II, 1996, pp. 1118-1119.

[26] Clyde Haberman, "A Medal both Coveted and Orphaned," *New York Times*, April 1, 2003, p. D1, at http://www.nytimes.com/2003/04/01/nyregion/nyc-a-medal-both-coveted-and-orphaned.html.

[27] Ibid.

In the FY1996 National Defense Authorization Act,[28] Congress enacted language that could significantly affect potential recipients. First, Congress waived the time limitation on any award or decoration for acts of valor during the Vietnam era[29] for actions in the Southeast Asia theater of operations. (Although the findings section of the language implies the language pertains to operations in the Ia Drang Valley, near Pleiku, South Vietnam, from October 23, 1965, to November 26, 1965, no such limitation appears in the waiver statement. Indeed, medals— including the MoH—were awarded for this action.)[30] Under this language, the Secretary concerned is instructed to review requests for consideration of awards/decorations, and to submit the following to the House National Security Committee and the Senate Armed Services Committee:

(A) A summary of the request consideration.

(B) The findings resulting from the review.

(C) The final action taken on the request for consideration.

Second, Congress waived the laws and regulations for awarding any decoration (including the Medal of Honor) for those so deserving who were serving in intelligence activities during the period January 1, 1940-December 31, 1990.[31] The Secretary of each military department was instructed to review each request for the award of a decoration during a one-year period commencing February 10, 1996. This was later extended to February 9, 1998.[32] The Secretary was further instructed to file a report with the House National Security Committee and Senate Armed Services Committee with respect to each request. The report is to contain:

(A) A summary of the request consideration.

(B) The findings resulting from the review.

(C) The final action taken on the request for consideration.

(D) Administrative or legislative recommendations to improve award procedures with respect to military intelligence personnel.

---

[28] P.L. 104-106, Sec. 522, February 10, 1996.

[29] "The term 'Vietnam era' means the period beginning on August 5, 1964, and ending on May 7, 1975." 38 U.S.C. 101(29).

[30] According to the commander of 1st Battalion, 7th Cavalry, a unit involved in combat at Ia Drang: I had been pushing my staff hard as we wrote letters of condolence to the families who had lost loved ones killed in action and prepared recommendations for medals and awards. We had problems on the awards: We had few who could type, so many of the forms were scrawled by hand by lantern light. Many witnesses had been evacuated with wounds or had already rotated for discharge. Too many men had died bravely and heroically, while the men who had witnessed their deeds had also been killed. Uncommon valor truly was a common virtue on the field at Landing Zone X-Ray those three days and two nights. Acts of valor that on other fields, on other days, would have been rewarded with the Medal of Honor or Distinguished Service Cross or a Silver Star were recognized only with a telegram saying "The Secretary of the Army regrets ..." Lt. Gen. Harold G. Moore and Joseph L. Galloway, *We Were Soldiers Once ... and Young, Ia Drang: The Battle that Changed the War in Vietnam* (New York: Random House, 1992), pp. 317-318.

[31] P.L. 104-106, Sec. 523, February 10, 1996.

[32] P.L. 105-85, Sec. 575, November 18, 1997.

These actions were taken in consideration of the fact that the records regarding intelligence activities are sealed for many years. Protecting this information for intelligence reasons means that those involved in intelligence activities are often ineligible to receive the Medal of Honor. In other words, should a person serving in intelligence perform an act of heroism worthy of the MoH, it is unlikely that the information could be publicly acknowledged. If the information is ever declassified, it is usually years after the fact. This delay could well mean that the individual who performed the act of heroism would be ineligible for the medal because of time on making recommendations.

Third, Congress waived the time requirements and other restrictions and then asked the Secretary of the Army and the Secretary of the Navy to review the records relating to the award of the Distinguished Service Cross and Navy Cross, respectively, awarded to Asian Americans or Native American Pacific Islanders who served during World War II.[33] The purpose of this review is to determine whether such awards should be upgraded to the Medal of Honor. The reasoning for this review is based on claims of discrimination that confronted Americans of Asian descent during the war. (For example, many Americans of Japanese descent were relocated to internment camps during the war.)

On October 12, 1998, it was reported that Army historians had completed a two-year search for Asian American recipients of the Distinguished Service Cross (DSC).[34] The names of 104 recipients (including Senator Daniel K. Inouye) were forwarded to a board of senior officers. This board considered if any of the forwarded recipients met the criteria for an upgrade to MoH. The list of those considered worthy of upgrading was then submitted to the President for final consideration. (The Navy determined that its sole Asian-American DSC recipient did not merit upgrading.) Proponents of the review/upgrading viewed this process as an overdue recognition of the heroics of these individuals long delayed by racism. Critics contend that the process was an act of "race-based political correctness" that diminished the value of the medal.[35]

Finally, Congress included a section entitled "Procedure for Consideration of Military Decorations Not Previously Submitted in Timely Fashion."[36] Under this section:

> (a) Upon request of a Member of Congress, the Secretary concerned shall review a proposal for the award or presentation of a decoration (or the upgrading of a decoration), either for an individual or a unit, that is not otherwise authorized to be presented or awarded due to limitations established by law or policy for timely submission of a recommendation for such award or presentation. Based on such review, the Secretary shall make a determination as to the merits of approving the award or presentation of the decoration and other determinations necessary to comply with subsection (b).

> (b) Upon making a determination under subsection (a) as to the merits of approving the award or presentation of the decoration, the Secretary concerned shall submit to the Committee on Armed Services of the Senate and the Committee on National Security of the House of Representatives and to the requesting member of Congress notice in writing of one of the following:

---

[33] P.L. 104-106, Sec. 524, February 10, 1996.

[34] Army Center of Military History, "U.S. Army Asian-Pacific Medal of Honor Recipients," at http://www.history.army.mil/html/topics/apam/ap-moh2.html.

[35] Martin Kasindorf, "Veterans Might Get Late Medals of Honor," *USA Today*, October 2, 1998, p. 2.

[36] P.L. 104-106, Sec. 526, February 10, 1996; 10 U.S.C. 1130

(1) The award or presentation of the decoration does not warrant approval on the merits.

(2) The award or presentation of the decoration warrants approval and a waiver by law of time restrictions prescribed by law is recommended.

(3) The award or presentation of the decoration warrants approval on the merits and has been approved as an exception to policy.

(4) The award or presentation of the decoration warrants approval on the merits, but a waiver of the time restrictions prescribed in law is not recommended.

A notice under paragraph (1) and (4) shall be accompanied by a statement of the reasons for the decision of the Secretary.[37]

Under this language Members of Congress will be able to directly request the Secretary to consider awarding military decorations. Although this allows Members to better serve their constituents as well as fulfill their constitutional duties in providing oversight, critics contend that it may unduly politicize the awards process.

In April 1996, despite restrictions on discussing awarding the Medal of Honor prematurely, the White House announced that it planned to award the medal to seven black soldiers who fought in World War II.[38] Although a number of Members of Congress[39] had been working in favor of awarding certain of these individuals' medals, the White House announced that these awards would be forthcoming. On May 13, 1996, the Senate included a section in its version of the FY1997 National Defense Authorization Act waiving the time limits for awarding the Medal of Honor to:

(1) Vernon J. Baker, who served as a first lieutenant in the 370th Infantry Regiment, 92nd Infantry Division.

(2) Edward A. Carter, who served as a staff sergeant in the 56th Armored Infantry Battalion, 12th Armored Division.

(3) John R. Fox, who served as a first lieutenant in the 366th Infantry Regiment, 92nd Infantry Division.

(4) Willy F. James, Jr., who served as a private first class in the 413th Infantry Regiment, 104th Infantry Division.

(5) Ruben Rivers, who served as a staff sergeant in the 761st Tank Battalion.

(6) Charles L. Thomas, who served as a first lieutenant in the 614th Tank Destroyer Battalion.

---

[37] U.S. Congress, House Conference Committee, *National Defense Authorization Act for Fiscal Year 1996*, 104th Cong., 2d sess., S. 1124, H.Rept. 104-450, January 22, 1996, pp. 133-134.

[38] Rick Weiss, "Seven Blacks in Line for Medal of Honor," *Washington Post*, April 28, 1996, p. A10.

[39] In the case of Ruben Rivers, his white commanding officer, David Williams, had sought for years to see that Rivers was awarded the Medal of Honor. After seeing to it that his unit received the Presidential Unit Citation in 1978, Williams was "[i]nvigorated by that victory [and] shifted his sights to Sergeant Rivers' Medal of Honor. Now, with the help of Sen. James Inhofe of Oklahoma and Members of the Congressional Black Caucus, victory is at hand." Joseph L. Galloway, "One Officer's 52-Year Quest," *U.S. News and World Report*, May 6, 1996, pp. 40-41.

(7) George Watson, who served as a private in the 29th Quartermaster Regiment.[40]

In the cases of Vernon J. Baker, Edward A. Carter, and Charles L. Thomas, their Medal of Honor pensions were awarded retroactively.[41]

On January 20, 1998, President Clinton awarded retired U.S. Marine Corps Major General James Day the Medal of Honor for his heroism as a Marine corporal during the battle for Okinawa in 1945. The original paperwork for his award was lost. Faded carbon copies of the recommendation surfaced in a fellow Marine's memorabilia and served as the basis for going forward with the award.[42]

Later in the same year, former U.S. Navy Hospital Corpsman Robert Ingram was awarded the Medal of Honor by President Clinton. Ingram's "comrades discovered at a 1995 reunion that he was alive and had never been decorated for his heroism...."[43] The Navy claimed to have lost the original paperwork. Following the congressionally mandated waiver of the time limits in November 1997, a review of Ingram's record resulted in the awarding of the medal.

In a symbolic gesture, then-President Reagan awarded the medal to the Vietnam veteran interred at the Tomb of the Unknowns in Arlington Cemetery in 1984. On May 14, 1998, the remains of the Vietnam veteran were exhumed. Advances in forensic identification using DNA testing allowed the military to positively identify the remains as those of Air Force 1st Lt. Michael Blassie, an A-37 pilot who was killed in the battle of An Loc, Vietnam, on May 11, 1972. His remains were returned to his family in Missouri. Family members sought to retain the medal awarded in 1984 by President Reagan. The request to retain the medal was denied. "[I]n a letter to the family..., Undersecretary of Defense Rudy de Leon said the Pentagon had decided that the medal had been a symbolic award to all service members who lost their lives in the conflict and not to any individual service member."[44]

"A decade-long effort by Congress to honor black war heroes had culminated in a strange result: Theodore Roosevelt, a famous white man, may soon receive the Medal of Honor—for a battle some historians say was won by black soldiers."[45] The efforts of historians searching for cases justifying the presentation of the award to black service members in the World Wars, and the legislation allowing Congress to waive time restraints for such and other cases, unearthed the controversy regarding Roosevelt. Under the time waiver Congress enacted in 1996, Representative Paul McHale introduced legislation requesting the President to award the MoH to then-Army Lt. Col. Theodore Roosevelt for his actions on July 1, 1898, in the attack of San Juan Heights, Cuba, during the Spanish-American War. Representative McHale argued that the Medal was not awarded because of resentment generated as a result of Roosevelt's criticism of the War Department.[46] Although it has been reported that the Army opposed presenting the MoH to

---

[40] P.L. 104-201, Sec. 561, September 23, 1996.

[41] P.L. 105-85, Sec. 577, November 18, 1997.

[42] Associated Press, "Marine General James L. Day, 73, Dies; Okinawa Battle Hero," *Washington Post*, November 2, 1998.

[43] Associated Press, "A 32-year Wait for the Medal of Honor," *Washington Post*, July 11, 1998, p. 3.

[44] Steve Vogel, "Medal Honoring 'Unknowns' Won't Go to Family of Identified Pilot," *Washington Post*, August 22, 1998, p. 5.

[45] Glenn R. Simpson, "Long Campaign to Get Teddy a Medal May Lead to a Slight of Black Heroes," *Wall Street Journal*, November 13, 1998, p. 1.

[46] *Congressional Record*, October 8, 1998, pp. H10121-10126.

Roosevelt, President Clinton signed the bill (H.R.2263) into law[47] and requested the Army to reconsider. Representatives of "Buffalo soldiers" claim that providing the award to Roosevelt would give him (Roosevelt) credit for "their success" in battle. Proponents contend this is an opportunity to amend a 100-year slight. Still others view this as the continuation of "identity politics" driving the awarding of the Medal of Honor.

Statutory Restrictions

In 1994, Congress passed P.L. 103-322 that stated:

> (a) In General.—Whoever knowingly wears, manufactures, or sells any decoration or medal authorized by Congress for the armed forces of the United States, or any of the service medals or badges awarded to the members of such forces, or the ribbon, button, or rosette of any such badge, decoration or medal, or any colorable imitation thereof, except when authorized under regulations made pursuant to law, shall be fined under this title [18 *U.S. Code* §704] or imprisoned not more than six months or both.

> (b) Congressional Medal of Honor.—

> (1) In General.—If a decoration or medal involved in an offense under subsection (a) is a Congressional Medal of Honor, in lieu of the punishment provided in that subsection, the offender shall be fined under this title, imprisoned not more than 1 year, or both.

> (2) Definitions.—(A) As used in subsection (a) with respect to a Congressional Medal of Honor, "sells" includes trades, barters, or exchanges for anything of value.[48]

The discharge certificate (DD 214) of a recipient of the Medal of Honor carries a notation of this award.

Stolen Valor Act

The Stolen Valor Act of 2005 was signed into law by President George W. Bush on December 20, 2006 (P.L. 109-437). The law made it a federal misdemeanor to falsely represent oneself as having received any U.S. military decoration or medal. If the decoration was the Medal of Honor, a defendant could be imprisoned up to one year if convicted. In 2007, Xavier Alvarez, an elected board member of a water district in Southern California, was charged with violating the law after stating at a public meeting that he was a recipient of the Medal of Honor after being wounded in action as a Marine. Alvarez declared that his remarks were protected speech under the First Amendment and that he should not be fined $5,000 for making a false claim.

---

[47] P.L. 105-371, November 12, 1998.

[48] This language was the result of changes created by P.L. 103-322, 108 Stat. 2113, September 13, 1994. This language increased the penalties to up to one year imprisonment and/or up to $100,000 fine for violations involving the Medal of Honor. Prior to this change, the law stated: Whoever knowingly wears, manufactures, or sells any decoration or medal authorized by Congress for the Armed Forces of the United States, or any of the service medals or badges awarded to the members of such forces, or the ribbon, button, or rosette of any such badge, decoration or medal, or any colorable imitation thereof, except when authorized under regulations made pursuant to law, shall be fined not more than $250 or imprisoned not more than six months, or both.

On June 28, 2012, in *United States v. Alvarez*, the U.S. Supreme Court overturned the original Stolen Valor Act of 2005 (6-3 decision), deeming it unconstitutional because it was, in the Justices' opinion, too broad in scope and violated the right of free speech. Justice Anthony M. Kennedy, who wrote the court's opinion, said the act "would endorse government authority to compile a list of subjects about which false statements are punishable."[49]

As a result of the Supreme Court decision, legislation was introduced in the 113th Congress to protect the reputation and meaning of the decoration. On June 3, 2013, President Obama signed H.R. 258, the Stolen Valor Act of 2013, into law (P.L. 113-32). This law now makes it "a federal crime for an individual to fraudulently hold oneself out to be a recipient of any of several specified military decorations or medals with the intent to obtain money, property, or other tangible benefit."[50] Violators could face up to a year in prison.

MoH Recipients in 2014

In the FY2002 National Defense Authorization Act (P.L. 107-107, Sec. 552), Congress called for a review of Jewish American and Hispanic American veteran war records from WWII, the Korean War, and the Vietnam War to ensure those deserving the Medal of Honor were not denied because of prejudice. During the review, records of several soldiers of neither Jewish nor Hispanic descent were also found to display criteria worthy of the Medal of Honor. The 2002 act was amended to allow these soldiers to be honored with the upgrade.

On March 18, 2014, President Obama presented Medals of Honor to 24 recipients, many of whom were overlooked initially due to racial bias because they were Hispanic, Jewish, or African American. He remarked that this was the single largest group of servicemembers to be awarded the Medal of Honor since the Second World War.[51] For full detail on all 24 recipients from WWII, Korea, and Vietnam, see the Valor 24 website at http://www.army.mil/medalofhonor/valor24/. According to a White House press release on February 21, 2014, "these veterans received the Medal of Honor in recognition of their valor during major combat operations in World War II, the Korean War and the Vietnam War. Each of these Soldiers' bravery was previously recognized by award of the Distinguished Service Cross, the nation's second highest military award; that award will be upgraded to the Medal of Honor in recognition of their gallantry, intrepidity and heroism above and beyond the call of duty."[52]

Additionally, the President awarded Medals of Honor to living recipients of the recent conflicts in Iraq and Afghanistan. On May 13, 2014, President Obama presented the U.S. military's highest award for valor to former Army Sergeant Kyle J. White for saving a soldier's life and helping evacuate other wounded soldiers during an ambush in Afghanistan in 2007. White received the

---

[49] *United States v. Alvarez*, Opinion by Justice Kennedy, June 28, 2012, p.11, Supreme Court of the United States at http://www.supremecourt.gov/opinions/11pdf/11-210d4e9.pdf.

[50] "Stolen Valor Act Becomes Law," Military.com, June 10, 2013, at http://www.military.com/military-report/stolen-valor-act-becomes-law.

[51] The White House Press Office, "Remarks by the President at Presentation Ceremony for the Medal of Honor," March 18, 2014, at http://www.whitehouse.gov/the-press-office/2014/03/18/remarks-president-presentation-ceremony-medal-honor.

[52] The White House Press Office, "President Obama to Award Medal of Honor," February 21, 2014, at http://www.whitehouse.gov/the-press-office/2014/02/21/president-obama-award-medal-honor.

Medal of Honor for his courageous actions during combat operations in Nuristan Province, Afghanistan.[53]

On June 19, 2014, President Obama presented retired Marine Corporal William "Kyle" Carpenter the Medal of Honor during a ceremony in the East Room of the White House. Carpenter received the medal for taking the blast from a grenade to protect fellow Marines, sustaining major wounds and surviving over 40 surgeries to repair a collapsed lung, fractured fingers, a shattered right arm, and multiple skin grafts.[54] Then on July 21, 2014, President Obama awarded in the name of Congress the Medal of Honor to Army Staff Sergeant Ryan M. Pitts. Pitts distinguished himself by extraordinary acts of heroism at the risk of his life while serving as a Forward Observer in 2d Platoon, Chosen Company, 2d Battalion (Airborne), 503d Infantry Regiment, 173d Airborne Brigade, during combat operations against an armed enemy at Vehicle Patrol Base Kahler in the vicinity of Wanat Village, Kunar Province, Afghanistan on July 13, 2008.[55] Sergeant Pitts is the ninth and most recent living recipient of the Medal of Honor from Afghanistan or Iraq.

Additional Sources of Information

CRS Report RL30011, *Medal of Honor Recipients: 1979-2013*, by Anne Leland

Congressional Medal of Honor Society at http://www.cmohs.org/

Department of Defense, U.S. Military Awards for Valor at http://valor.defense.gov/

DOD Knowledge Base, Boards for Correction of Military Records at https://kb.defense.gov/app/answers/detail/a_id/386/~/boards-for-correction-of-military-records

U.S. Army, Valor 24 website at http://www.army.mil/medalofhonor/valor24/

---

[53] The White House Blog, "President Obama Awards the Medal of Honor to Sgt. Kyle J. White," May 13, 2014, at http://www.whitehouse.gov/blog/2014/05/13/president-obama-awards-medal-honor-sgt-kyle-j-white.

[54] The White House Blog, "President Obama Awards the Medal of Honor to Corporal William "Kyle" Carpenter," June 19, 2014, at http://www.whitehouse.gov/blog/2014/06/19/president-awards-medal-honor-corporal-william-kyle-carpenter.

[55] The White House Press Office, "Remarks by the President at Presentation of the Medal of Honor to Staff Sergeant Ryan Pitts," July 21, 2014, at http://www.whitehouse.gov/the-press-office/2014/07/21/remarks-president-presentation-medal-honor-staff-sergeant-ryan-pitts.

Appendix.

Citations

Below are samples of official MoH citations. (An * asterisk indicates a posthumous award.)

Coates, Jefferson

Rank and organization: Corporal, Company I, 14th Michigan Infantry. *Place and date:* At Gettysburg, PA, 1 July 1863. *Entered service at:* Boscobel, Wis. *Birth:* Grant County, Wis. *Date of issue:* 29 June 1866. *Citation:* Unsurpassed courage in battle, where he had both eyes shot out.

Edgerton, Nathan H.

Rank and organization: Lieutenant and Adjutant, 6th United States Colored Troops. *Place and date:* At Chapins Farm, VA, 29 September 1864. *Entered service:* At Philadelphia, PA. *Birth:* ____. *Date of issue:* 30 March 1898. *Citation:* Took up the flag after three color bearers had been shot down and bore forward, though himself wounded.

*Roosevelt, Theodore

Rank and organization: Lieutenant Colonel, U.S. Army. *Place and date*: At San Juan Hill, 1 July 1898. *Date of issue*: 16 January 2001. *Citation*: Lieutenant Colonel Theodore Roosevelt distinguished himself by acts of bravery on 1 July, 1898, near Santiago de Cuba, Republic of Cuba, while leading a daring charge up San Juan Hill. Lieutenant Colonel Roosevelt, in total disregard for his personal safety, and accompanied by only four or five men, led a desperate and gallant charge up San Juan Hill, encouraging his troops to continue the assault through withering enemy fire over open countryside. Facing the enemy's heavy fire, he displayed extraordinary bravery throughout the charge, and was the first to reach the enemy trenches, where he quickly killed one of the enemies with his pistol, allowing his men to continue the assault. His leadership and valor turned the tide in the Battle for San Juan Hill. Lieutenant Colonel Roosevelt's extraordinary heroism and devotion to duty are in keeping with the highest traditions of military service and reflect great credit upon himself, his unit, and the United States Army.[56]

*Flaherty, Francis C.

Rank and organization: Ensign, U.S. Naval Reserve. *Born:* 15 March 1919, Charlotte, Mich. *Accredited to:* Michigan. *Citation:* For conspicuous devotion to duty and extraordinary courage and complete disregard of his own life, above and beyond the call of duty, during the attack on Pearl Harbor, by Japanese forces on 7 December 1941. When it was seen that the *USS Oklahoma* was going to capsize and the order was given to abandon ship, Ensign Flaherty remained in a

---

[56] "Theodore Roosevelt," Congressional Medal of Honor Society at http://www.cmohs.org/recipient-detail/2178/roosevelt-theodore.php and P.L. 105-371. For additional background information, see "Remarks on Presenting the Medal of Honor," January 16, 2001 by President Bill Clinton at http://www.presidency.ucsb.edu/ws/index.php?pid=64177&st=medal+of+honor&st1=roosevelt and the National Archives *Prologue* magazine article, "I Am Entitled to the Medal of Honor and I Want It: Theodore Roosevelt and His Quest for Glory," by Mitchell Yockelson, Spring 1998, at http://www.archives.gov/publications/prologue/1998/spring/roosevelt-and-medal-of-honor-1.html.

turret, holding a flashlight so the remainder of the turret crew could escape, thereby sacrificing his own life.

*Gilmore, Howard Walter

Rank and organization: Commander, U.S. Navy. *Born:* 29 September 1902, Selma, Ala. *Appointed from:* Louisiana. *Other Navy award:* Navy Cross with one gold star. *Citation:* For distinguished gallantry and valor above and beyond the call of duty as Commanding Officer of the *USS Growler* during her Fourth War Patrol in the Southwest Pacific from 10 January to 7 February 1943. Boldly striking at the enemy in spite of continuous hostile air and anti-submarine patrols, Commander Gilmore sank one Japanese freighter and damaged another by torpedo fire, successfully evading severe depth charges following each attack. In the darkness of night on 7 February, enemy gunboat closed range and prepared to ram the *Growler*. Commander Gilmore daringly maneuvered to avoid the crash and rammed the attacker instead, ripping into her port side at 17 knots and bursting wide her plates. In the terrific fire of the sinking gunboat's heavy machine guns, Commander Gilmore calmly gave the order to clear the bridge, and refusing safety for himself, remained on the deck while his men preceded him below. Struck down by the fusillade of bullets and having done his utmost against the enemy, in his final living moments, Commander Gilmore gave his last order to the officer of the deck, "Take her down." The *Growler* dived; seriously damaged but under control, she was brought safely to port by her well-trained crew inspired by the courageous fighting spirit of their dead captain.

*Bobo, John P.

Rank and organization: Second Lieutenant, United States Marine Corps Reserve, 3rd Battalion, 9th Marines, 3rd Marine Division (Rein) FMF. *Place and date:* Quang Tri Province, Republic of Vietnam, 30 March 1967. *Entered service at:* Buffalo, N.Y. *Date and place of birth:* February 14, 1943, Niagara Falls, N.Y. *Citation:* For conspicuous gallantry and intrepidity at the risk of his life above and beyond the call of duty. Company I was establishing night ambush sites when the command group was attacked by a reinforced North Vietnamese company supported by heavy automatic weapons and mortar fire. Lieutenant Bobo immediately organized a hasty defense and moved from position to position encouraging the outnumbered Marines despite the murderous enemy fire. Recovering a rocket launcher from among friendly casualties, he organized a new launcher team and directed its fire into the enemy machine gun positions. When an exploding enemy mortar round severed Lieutenant Bobo's right leg below the knee, he refused to be evacuated and insisted upon being placed in a firing position to cover the movement of the command group to a better location. With a web belt around his leg serving as a tourniquet and with his leg jammed into the dirt to curtail the bleeding, he remained in this position and delivered devastating fire into the ranks of the enemy attempting to overrun the Marines. Lieutenant Bobo was mortally wounded while firing his weapon into the main point of the enemy attack but his valiant spirit inspired his men to heroic efforts, and his tenacious stand enabled the command group to gain a protective position where it repulsed the enemy onslaught. Lieutenant Bobo's superb leadership, dauntless courage, and bold initiative reflected great credit upon himself and upheld the highest traditions of the Marine Corps and the United States Naval Service. He gallantly gave his life for his country.

*Smith, Paul R.

Rank and Organization: Sergeant First Class, United States Army. For conspicuous gallantry and intrepidity at the risk of his life above and beyond the call of duty. Sergeant First Class Paul R.

Smith distinguished himself by acts of gallantry and intrepidity above and beyond the call of duty in action with an armed enemy near Baghdad International Airport, Baghdad, Iraq on 4 April 2003. On that day, Sergeant First Class Smith was engaged in the construction of a prisoner of war holding area when his Task Force was violently attacked by a company-sized enemy force. Realizing the vulnerability of over 100 fellow soldiers, Sergeant First Class Smith quickly organized a hasty defense consisting of two platoons of soldiers, one Bradley Fighting Vehicle and three armored personnel carriers. As the fight developed, Sergeant First Class Smith braved hostile enemy fire to personally engage the enemy with hand grenades and anti-tank weapons, and organized the evacuation of three wounded soldiers from an armored personnel carrier struck by a rocket propelled grenade and a 60mm mortar round. Fearing the enemy would overrun their defenses, Sergeant First Class Smith moved under withering enemy fire to man a .50 caliber machine gun mounted on a damaged armored personnel carrier. In total disregard for his own life, he maintained his exposed position in order to engage the attacking enemy force. During this action, he was mortally wounded. His courageous actions helped defeat the enemy attack, and resulted in as many as 50 enemy soldiers killed, while allowing the safe withdrawal of numerous wounded soldiers. Sergeant First Class Smith's extraordinary heroism and uncommon valor are in keeping with the highest traditions of the military service and reflect great credit upon himself, the Third Infantry Division "Rock of the Marne," and the United States Army.

*Kapaun, Emil Joseph

Rank and Organization: Captain (Chaplain), United States Army. For conspicuous gallantry and intrepidity at the risk of his life above and beyond the call of duty while serving with the 3d Battalion, 8th Cavalry Regiment, 1st Cavalry Division, during combat operations against an armed enemy at Unsan, Korea, from November 1-2, 1950. On November 1, as Chinese Communist Forces viciously attacked friendly elements, Chaplain Kapaun calmly walked through withering enemy fire in order to provide comfort and medical aid to his comrades and rescue friendly wounded from no-man's land. Though the Americans successfully repelled the assault, they found themselves surrounded by the enemy. Facing annihilation, the able-bodied men were ordered to evacuate. However, Chaplain Kapaun, fully aware of his certain capture, elected to stay behind with the wounded. After the enemy succeeded in breaking through the defense in the early morning hours of November 2, Chaplain Kapaun continually made rounds, as hand-to-hand combat ensued. As Chinese Communist Forces approached the American position, Chaplain Kapaun noticed an injured Chinese officer amongst the wounded and convinced him to negotiate the safe surrender of the American Forces. Shortly after his capture, Chaplain Kapaun, with complete disregard for his personal safety and unwavering resolve, bravely pushed aside an enemy soldier preparing to execute Sergeant First Class Herbert A. Miller. Not only did Chaplain Kapaun's gallantry save the life of Sergeant Miller, but also his unparalleled courage and leadership inspired all those present, including those who might have otherwise fled in panic, to remain and fight the enemy until captured. Chaplain Kapaun's extraordinary heroism and selflessness, above and beyond the call of duty, are in keeping with the highest traditions of military service and reflect great credit upon himself, the 3d Battalion, 8th Cavalry Regiment, the 1st Cavalry Division, and the United States Army.[57] President Barack Obama presented the Medal of Honor to Kapaun's nephew at the White House on April 11, 2013.[58]

---

[57] "Kapaun, Emil Joseph," Congressional Medal of Honor Society at http://www.cmohs.org/recipient-detail/3483/kapaun-kapaun-joseph.php.

[58] "Remarks by the President at Presentation of the Medal of Honor to Chaplain Emil J. Kapaun, U.S. Army," The White House, Office of the Press Secretary, May 11, 2013, at http://www.whitehouse.gov/the-press-office/ (continued...)

Pitts, Ryan M.

Rank and Organization: Sergeant, United States Army. For conspicuous gallantry and intrepidity at the risk of his life above and beyond the call of duty:[59]

Sergeant Ryan M. Pitts distinguished himself by extraordinary acts of heroism at the risk of his life above and beyond the call of duty while serving as a Forward Observer in 2d Platoon, Chosen Company, 2d Battalion (Airborne), 503d Infantry Regiment, 173d Airborne Brigade, during combat operations against an armed enemy at Vehicle Patrol Base Kahler vicinity of Wanat Village, Kunar Province, Afghanistan on July 13, 2008. Early that morning, while Sergeant Pitts was providing perimeter security at Observation Post Topside, a well-organized Anti-Afghan Force consisting of over 200 members initiated a close proximity sustained and complex assault using accurate and intense rocket-propelled grenade, machine gun and small arms fire on Wanat Vehicle Patrol Base. An immediate wave of rocket-propelled grenade rounds engulfed the Observation Post wounding Sergeant Pitts and inflicting heavy casualties. Sergeant Pitts had been knocked to the ground and was bleeding heavily from shrapnel wounds to his arm and legs, but with incredible toughness and resolve, he subsequently took control of the observation post and returned fire on the enemy. As the enemy drew nearer, Sergeant Pitts threw grenades, holding them after the pin was pulled and the safety lever was released to allow a nearly immediate detonation on the hostile forces. Unable to stand on his own and near death because of the severity of his wounds and blood loss, Sergeant Pitts continued to lay suppressive fire until a two-man reinforcement team arrived. Sergeant Pitts quickly assisted them by giving up his main weapon and gathering ammunition all while continually lobbing fragmentary grenades until these were expended. At this point, Sergeant Pitts crawled to the northern position radio and described the situation to the command post as the enemy continued to try and isolate the Observation Post from the main Patrol Base. With the enemy close enough for him to hear their voices and with total disregard for his own life, Sergeant Pitts whispered in radio situation reports and conveyed information that the Command Post used to provide indirect fire support. Sergeant Pitts' courage, steadfast commitment to the defense of his unit and ability to fight while seriously wounded prevented the enemy from overrunning the observation post and capturing fallen American soldiers, and ultimately prevented the enemy from gaining fortified positions on higher ground from which to attack Wanat Vehicle Patrol Base. Sergeant Ryan M. Pitts' extraordinary heroism and selflessness above and beyond the call of duty are in keeping with the highest traditions of military service and reflect great credit upon himself, Company C, 2d Battalion (Airborne), 503d Infantry Regiment, 173d Airborne Brigade and the United States Army.

(...continued)

2013/04/11/remarks-president-presentation-medal-honor-chaplain-emil-j-kapaun-us-arm.

[59] U.S. Army, Official Citation for the Medal of Honor, Staff Sergeant Ryan Pitts, Operation Enduring Freedom, July 21, 2014, at http://www.army.mil/medalofhonor/pitts/profile/index.html.

Table A-1. Medal of Honor Breakdown by War and Service

(as of July 23, 2014)

War	Total Awards	Army	Navy	Marines	Air Force	Coast Guard	Posthumous	Civilian	Air Corps
Civil War	1,522	1,198	307	17			29	(2) Navy (2) Army	
Indian Campaigns	426	426					12	(4) Army	
Korea 1871	15		9	6					
Spanish American	110	31	64	15			1		
Samoa	4		1	3					
Philippine Insurrection	80	69	5	6			4		
Philippine Outlaws	6	1	5						
Boxer Rebellion	59	4	22	33			1		
Mexican Campaign	56	1	46	9					
Haiti	6			6					
Dominican Republic	3			3					
World War I	124	95	21	8			33		Army (4)
Haiti 1919-1920	2			2					
Nicaraguan Campaign	2			2					
World War II	471	331	57	82		1	273		Army (37)
Korean War	145	92	7	42	4		107		
Vietnam	256	169	16	57	14		161		
Somalia	2	2					2		
Afghanistan	11	8	1	2			3		
Iraq	4	2	1	1			4		
Non-Combat	193	3	185	5			5		Army (1)
Unknowns	9	9					9		
TOTALS	3,507	2,441	747	299	18	1	644		

Notes: Updated data provided to CRS courtesy of the Congressional Medal of Honor Society. These totals reflect the total number of Medals of Honor awarded. Nineteen (19) men received a second award. Fourteen (14) of these men received two (2) for separate actions, five (5) received the Navy and Army Medals for Honor for the same action. The Air Corps was the predecessor of the U.S. Air Force from 1926-1947 and known officially as the Army Air Corps according to the "Centennial of Army Aviation" at http://www.army.mil/aviation/aircorps/.

Table A-2. Medal of Honor Total Numbers

(As of July 23, 2014)

Total Medals of Honor Awarded	3,507
Total Numbers of Recipients	3,488
Total Number of Double Recipients	19
Total Number of Living Recipients	78

Source: Congressional Medal of Honor Society.

Author Contact Information

David F. Burrelli
Specialist in Military Manpower Policy
dburrelli@crs.loc.gov, 7-8033

Barbara Salazar Torreon
Information Research Specialist
btorreon@crs.loc.gov, 7-8996

www.ingramcontent.com/pod-product-compliance
Lightning Source LLC
Chambersburg PA
CBHW080759290526
45790CB00008B/3512